Your Marriage & Family

LIKE NO OTHER

Your Marriage Like No Other

Your Marriage Like No Other

REHOBOTH HOUSE™

YOUR MARRIAGE AND FAMILY LIKE NO OTHER
Leaving A Legacy For Your Generation

Copyright © 2018 By Christy Uche

All Rights Reserved

ISBN: 978-1-64301-008-3

This book is published in the United States of America by Rehoboth House, Chicago and printed by permission in Nigeria by Rehoboth Publishing, Lagos.

The opinions expressed by the author in this book are exclusively hers and not those of Rehoboth House.

No part of this publication may be reproduced, transmitted or stored in any retrieval system without a written permission of the author who is the legal copyright owner, except for brief quotations and reviews for personal and group Bible studies. The use of short quotations or occasional page copying for personal or group study is also permitted and encouraged to stregnthen and build strong families.

All Scripture quotations are taken from the Kings James Version of the Bible, unless otherwise indicated.

Forward enquiries to Christy Uche for teachings, seminars and workshops on Family and Relationship: wimmpray@yahoo.com or call +234 803 708 6437

Placing Online Orders for the Book Visit
amazon.com, barnesandnoble.com and other online bookstores.

Interior and Cover Designed by Rehoboth House, Chicago
www.rehobothhouseonline.com
email:info@rehobothhouseonline.com

First Print, July 2018

Printed in the Federal Republic of Nigeria by Permission
By Rehoboth Publishing, 174 Ikorodu Road, Lagos
Tel: 234-802-304-3072
E-mail: rehobothpublishing@gmail.com

REHOBOTH HOUSE

Your Marriage Like No Other

Table of Contents

Dedication..ix

Acknowledgment..xi

Introduction...xiii

CHAPTER ONE

Uniqueness A Divine Arrangement..1

CHAPTER TWO

The Angle Of Comparison..5

CHAPTER THREE

Why Marriages And Families Are Different.......................................15

CHAPTER FOUR

Understanding Factor..29

CHAPTER FIVE

Issues Of Submission...39

CHAPTER SIX

Tidy Up Your Home...45

CHAPTER SEVEN

My Story..55

Your Marriage Like No Other

Dedication

I humbly dedicate this book to the Holy Spirit who leads and makes our marriage like no other. God is helping us to successfully navigate through our marriage life by His wisdom, understanding and divine strength. To Him alone be all the glory.

Your Marriage Like No Other

Your Marriage X *Like No Other*

Acknowledgment

I bless God that this book is out to His glory and that it will serve as therapy and solution to anyone that has been ordained to come in contact with it.

Thank you, my dear husband, you are the reason for all these good things that God is doing in our family. You saw me as the best gift ever, your protection and warmth are second to none, you provided an enabling environment for me to excel, you are always available to help. You are my crown, my glory, and my joy. You will ever be remembered by heaven and eat the fruit thereof. In all the gates you shall be called blessed. I love you Obim.

Joel my grandson (as I fondly call you) fought to make this story complete, and your name shall be greatly announced at the mountaintop.

Enyichi, you are a gift to me, you were created to be my divine and destiny helper. I love you, and the forces of heaven must reward your tireless efforts. Blessed are those that make life and work easy for me, Apostle Glory Aaron, Mommy Constance, Chosen, Amaka, National Executives, Marks & Angels Boutique, Joy Chidiebere, Dr. Amaka, Anele, Ngozi Chibuiko, Mommy Chionye, Mommy Ngozi Innocent, Miriam Udealor, Mommy Eudora and all Gethsemane Committee members, my driver and a host of other Potter's House Women that has volunteered themselves to sacrifice in our lives. The state and leaders of Potter's House Women I salute your efforts both past and present.

Our children Amby, Samuel, Stella, and Progress, you all are receipt and reward of our ministry. The mantle is ready on you. Thank you all for your love and sacrifice, it is awesome, and it has kept us going.

God bless you all.

Introduction

Two wise hearted individuals make a good marriage. As a child, I desired and envisioned a good marriage and a sweet home, as I watched and saw the experiences of a sweet home. I disliked homes that were not functioning well and stamped my feet to show my dislike, each time I came across one.

Looking around me then, I also noticed that each marriage differs from the other in many ways. I remembered that our nearest neighbor was a single parent family with grown-up children. She struggled alone with little or no help, but ours was a growing and dynamic family. I was the eldest among my siblings my father was there like a lion who vehemently decided what happens while my mother didn't have much to contribute. Even if she did, her contributions was viewed as insignificant and not appreciated.

The ministry of the Potter's House Women Fellowship International has exposed and widened my understanding of life and marriage. My involvement in the corridors of power mainly amongst women has also defined my perspective on this matter. How I wish my parents were still alive to watch, as I evolve and read this book full of simple to understand insights and nuggets.

From the first time I entered into my marriage, right from the beginning of our engagement to date, I can confidently say my marriage is different. We both work together towards building a solid, peaceful, dynamic and prosperous home.

My first meeting with my husband was in the corner of our neighbor's house. Before that meeting, I had a series of encounters that defined the kind of man who was coming into my life due to the purposes of God for my future. God arranged my marriage so much so that friends around me got the revelation and everything worked out divinely. My story is different, my husband's giving styles were different, my friends would come with things their fiancés had bought for them, but mine was different.

Events that took place during our courtship were strictly different based on the beliefs of our church and fellowship then. I did not see any of my brother or sisters-in-law to be

Introduction

during our courtship because we cannot go too close to each other as an unmarried couple.

During our traditional marriage rites, some of our guests had a car accident on their way home that changed the whole story after our traditional rites. On getting to my husband's house that cool evening after the reception, our best man began to prophesy, and those words are etched in our hearts and serve as the masterpiece of God's program for our lives.

This book came to add a voice to the existing family books so that each man and woman should know what works best for them in the light of love, maturity, and fulfillment of their assignment in God. You may be wondering what is wrong with your marriage. Probably you have not gotten the right key and how to use it to explore the hidden treasure in your marriage and family.

1 Peter 3:1-2 turned my marriage on the right direction, it put things in proper perspective, and now we are reaping the benefit of obedience.

> *"Likewise, ye wives, be in subjection to your husbands; that, if any obey not the word, they also may without the word be won by the conversation of the wives; While they behold your chaste conversation coupled with fear. Whose*

adorning let it not be that outward adorning of plaiting the hair, and of wearing of gold, or of putting on of apparel."

You cannot build a strong marriage without the word of God as the foundation. The revelation of each word builds a successful home where peace, joy, and abundance are experienced. As you watch and admire other people's homes, know that your home is like no other. Your marriage and family shall be everlasting memories if you read and obey the words of the Lord.

More so, you are encouraged to seek God, study your spouse and your environment

Know where you started from, where you are at each time and where you are heading to

A purposeless marriage has no plan and has nothing to guide them or to focus on

Have a strong determination to make your marriage work. That entails leaving your egos behind, and selfishness should be abhorred aggressively

Two of you must join forces to fight against every mountain of opposition. Always be ready to pay the price for peace.

Give time for maturity and growth. Understanding will help

Introduction

both of you walk together in times and seasons of turbulence for two are better than one

Two of you may not be at the same phase or level of understanding at the same time. Perception and perspective may differ, but patience and love will bridge the gap

Coming together is a beginning, staying together is a process, walking together is a success.

There are several teachings on marriage prevalent these days, based on tradition, culture or the teacher's revelation, philosophy, religious background, beliefs, and interpretation. Be careful how you interact with those teachings, less you tear your home apart with your hands. A lot of those teachings have torn many homes apart, stolen their joy and enslaved them. Therefore, I say prayerfully, WATCH!

> *"Jesus answered: "Watch out that no one deceives you" (Matthew 24:4 NIV).*

The principles of marriage as intended by God are the same and universal, but the application differs from generation to generation and from family to family. In your marriage, apply understanding and wisdom and shun unnecessary competition and emulation. Know what works for you, do the best you can for your family so that they will have pleasant memories of you when you are no more. Each couple and family has to sincerely examine themselves and know what they lack and be willing to make the necessary adjustments to make up for what is lacking it. Strengthen the bars of your gates and encourage each other. The truth is that there are prices and sacrifices to make for your family and marriage. Selfishness, ego, and pride should be avoided to save your home. Do everything to allow peace, joy, progress, and harmony to be established and sustained in your home for the benefit of all. Know that your children, family and the society will reward you for every sacrifice you make to save your posterity and inheritance.

Chapter One

Uniqueness: A Divine Arrangement

The activities of the day were coming to a close, but Elisa's heart beats, what would become of me, how would my night be? The cloud was fizzling out, the evening glow was rising, and darkness begins to appear in the sky but a certain house was filled with uncertainty, the atmosphere was dreadful, children were hiding, and their heart's panting. Were they expecting a stranger, an influence or a monster? No is the answer. The lion of the house (the father and husband) is coming back; different kinds of thoughts are flowing through their minds rehearsing possible questions and answers. The house is quiet as the graveyard, no pin falls because the lion is coming home ready to roar. Who knows what the family of this supposed lion of the house taught him as a young man or the culture and tradition he grew up from, or the influence of his friends and his colleagues has on him that inspire him to act like the "Okonkwo of the Things Fall Apart"? The truth of the matter is that pictures and images of this family pattern leave a lasting memory on the wife and children.

In the family and marriage of Mr. Obichukwu, things are working out differently. The children look out for the coming back of their hero (their father) with anticipation and expression of excitement. His presence brings hope and joy like a stream in the desert and like dew upon a tender plant. He comes home to meet a royal welcome, and a table set royally for the king of the house.

Some families have no children, but they still enjoy their union and hope for the best while childlessness has divided many families.

Some families are monogamous, polygamous, polyandry or single parenting, etc. Whatever be your situation never commit suicide, feel depressed or abandoned.

> "There's hope of a tree if it is cut down, that it will sprout again, and the tender branch thereof will not cease." (Job 14: 7).

Uniqueness: A Divine Arrangement

Your marriage is like no other. Many people view widowhood as a better option because of the bitter and unexpected experiences in their marriage journey.

Lately, I have had series of calls and witnessed people who marriage had dealt with resulting to depression, mental disorder, and devastated futures, Some are left confused, sad, resentful, regretful, guilty and abandoned. Failed marriage negatively affects everyone concerned, and it is one of the greatest disappointments in life. Most people have lost focus, identity, joy, and purpose and are miserable than ever because of how they handle the challenges of marriage.

Some group of women went out on evangelism after our fellowship on a Saturday. Eventually, they met a certain woman and began to preach the gospel to her. The woman exclaimed courteously and said "Can children of God be so good looking and sophisticated like you all are? She went further and said, 'I thought they used to be haggard, beggars and nonentities." When the gospel gripped her heart, she began to confess why she is into prostitution. According to her, she went into prostitution as revenge against her husband's infidelity. She said although she was a Christian previously, but when she discovered that her husband was cheating on her to the extent of having a child outside their matrimonial home, she abandoned her husband and left her marriage to live in the brothel with her daughter. What madness! This woman studied Criminology at Ahmadu Bellow University, Zaria. Looking at her, you could see frustration, feeling of total abandonment, rejection and lack of proper coordination. We have met similar cases like that, and it's heartbreaking to see a waste of human resources. See what the Bible says in Proverbs. 6:32,

> *"But whoso committeth adultery with a woman lacketh understanding: he that doeth it destroyeth his own soul."*

This woman has lost focus and identity.

> *"The man that wandereth out of the way of understanding shall remain in the congregation of the dead" (Prov. 21:16).*

No one ever dreams of a failed marriage nor prayed for it, but it's always there when the couple fails to understand themselves properly and sincerely confront the realities on the ground before it gets out of hand. We must note and appreciate that two persons are involved in any marriage relationship and need respect for each other despite the age difference, family background, academic and socioeconomic status, etc. Every spouse should look into their marriage and find out what it lacks. Anyone more equipped can supply what is needed to keep the marriage alive, for the good of every member of the family. Never allow anything, anybody, no matter who or what to tear your marriage apart. You must pay every price to keep your marriage and family healthy and strong.

Chapter Two

The Angle Of Comparison

No two marriages are the same. Therefore, there is no need for comparison. To be candid, any form of unhealthy comparison is not of God and does not depict the fruit of the Holy Spirit. Even as an individual you must acknowledge that you are unique, you are not like anybody else. Your marriage is not like nobody's marriage; your destiny is not like nobody's. Our whole destiny is about heaven, but our personality and interest differ.

So, there is no reason to embarrass ourselves. Sometimes because of comparison people prefer the other person's spouse than theirs and feel offended over the insignificant issues of life. They bear malice and seek revenge without remorse. Because of this, the joy and love in marriage are traded or lost due to the mere comparison.

Dictionary says to compare means "to assess the similarities and differences between two or more things." You know when you want to compare two marriages, you will attempt to access some information that is not readily available on the surface. To access means "to look into, to investigate, to use means in others to find out the result." You are trying to evaluate or assess the two to find out their difference and similarities.

So If you want to examine or investigate the similarities in others to compare the two variables between your marriage and theirs, you realize that you will need to go into a thorough investigation. At this point, you become conscious of the other person's spouse and starts seeing the details that ordinarily you would not have noticed. If another person's spouse passes by, you will check him in and out. Compare every detail possible to ascertain the difference between the person and your spouse. At this point, the devil has scored his number one card against you. Please, let your desire and focus be on your spouse and be ready to accept him or her for

The Angle Of Comparison

who they are. Unacceptability experienced in many homes is as a result of the unhealthy comparison that has destroyed the fabrics of many marriages and homes.

A lady came back from work and was complaining that her husband is not as caring as her colleague's husband. She tells her husband how the other man comes to drive his wife home, carries her bag, gives her kiss and hugs her, opens the door of their car for her and because of this, she starts a quarrel with her husband simply because he is not behaving like the colleague's spouse. Not knowing that the man that picks his wife at the same time was in an illicit relationship with the girlfriend of his wife. The day their relationship was revealed, everybody was stunned, shouting; "how can this good man be this treacherous?"

Sometimes because of lack of understanding, we waste valuable time trying to check and balance a fruitless venture comparing x with y. Someone said, my husband has never done a birthday party for me; I have never been celebrated in this house as my friends. She complained that the husband doesn't even remember her birthday. Just know that families differ. Someone called me and said I should talk to her husband and persuade him to pay back the money he borrowed from her. She said the husband used the money to take her out. When they came back, she asked her husband to pay back the money, but her husband refused and said that he used the money in taking her out. Never allow needless things to bring the family to a standstill, give peace a chance, you will still enjoy.

I have sat down to examine all my children and observed that they are all important, and unique in one way or the other. I also realize that they have weaknesses to deal with. So the best thing I do is to treat every one of them according to their uniqueness and bring the best out of them. This is not just applicable to marriage; it applies to everything about life. Even the people you teach, you should know that they have something in them that you don't have, and you have what they don't have. So, it's a symbiotic relationship.

God created us to be unique, and that uniqueness is divine equipment to enable us to fulfill God's purposes for our lives. Open your heart to accept people the way they are. In comparison, you waste a lot of time comparing people. Somebody said, "if you want to work with people just look at their strength and work with it."

THE EVIL OF COMPARISON

Comparison can cause anxiety because after comparing you will put yourself under pressure to be better than the person you compared yourself with. It brings jealousy and envy.

The Angle Of Comparison

Somebody told me that he saw someone who would have married her and the man is very wealthy presently while her husband lives in penury. It is better to marry someone who accepts you and respects your purpose than marrying vain imagination. You will lose a lot when you are comparing.

Comparison brings about complaining and murmuring. When you find out about the difference in another home, you will be whispering it from one person to the other to find out if your findings are correct or not. It breeds grudges and regrets; you will be saying had I known I wouldn't have married this person. It blinds one's eyes to the good in one's spouse and denies you the associated benefits and fruits.

Whoever you are, accept yourself, accept your spouse and the children God has given you, your family is like no other. Be confident of who you are in God. However, that should not stop you from improving yourself and making every effort to be relevant.

One of the remedies of comparison is to determine that your marriage will not fail. If you see what is threatening or even destroying your marriage, (maybe your spouse has not seen it), begin to ask God for mercy and the wisdom to practically confront the issues. Most time asking people to pray for your marriage may not be the best, it can make it worse.

Appreciate your marriage and the uniqueness of your family and make the best of it. If you are a single girl, appreciate your uniqueness and serve God and humanity to the fullest. Don't be envious when you see married women and start bemoaning "if only I am married." Your time is coming, wait patiently and build a godly character that will attract your God-ordained man. If you are a widow, appreciate your uniqueness and make the best out of it and thank God that He knows the best for you. If you are a single parent, divorced, a widow/widower, whatever is your marital status now, make the best you can for yourself, do something that will make people commend you and say that yours is the best. If your family is without a child, find something good to rejoice about and keep moving on in life. Endeavour to make the best of every situation you find yourself.

The uniqueness of your marriage needs God's divine help and direction. It needs the grace of God. The issue of family uniqueness must be acknowledged. Find out what God has called your marriage to accomplish. There is no family or marriage without a purpose to fulfill in God. There are families called to pastor people and feed them spiritually while some are called to help, feed and meet the needs of people and the Body of Christ financially. Some families are called to mentor, train and grow other people's children and bring them to

The Angle Of Comparison

sonship. *Find out the purposes of your marriage on earth because if you don't discover it, your family will not be properly positioned. There will be no satisfaction or fruit or reward now and in the days to come, even in eternity.*

Keep focus: Keep your eyes on what God has called you and your family to do. Focus on your uniqueness. Don't look at another person's family. Don't let your eyes deceive you. Your marriage is like no other. What brings comparison is when your eyes are on others. Most time you see people laughing outside, but inside, they in troubled, mourning, weeping and lamenting. If your focus is on another person's marriage, family and children you will be in anguish and live in regret always. For instance, you will be complaining that their children are doing better than yours, and putting unnecessary pressure on your children, instead of encouraging and correcting them in love.

There is something that my son Samuel posted on his Facebook page, "If your child is not taking the first position in the class, find out, there are other things he can do better." What he is simply saying is that if your child is not good in an area, please don't push him, rather find out where he is good at. That child may be good at football, or something else. There is something very child is good at. One person may be good at science the other that in arts. As a parent, you guide them through to accomplish what they are good at. For instance, my daughter wants to study pharmacy, I looked at her and told her that you could not do pharmacy. You can't sit down for a long time reading; rather you are skillful in using your hands. Your children are unique, that is the wisdom of God. No spouse or child is hundred percent (100%) complete. Just know that change is a process. You must give change a chance and time to work for visible and realistic positive change. Nobody changes automatically. Characters are built over time. It needs patience and discipline. Build on the area that will encourage your spouse. Focus on his/her strength and pray over his/her weakness. Nagging, violence, quarrying, verbal abuse, fighting complaining and murmuring cannot change a man. But patience with your spouse. Prayers, tolerance, meekness and quiet spirit can influence change in his life.

> *"Likewise, ye wives, be in subjection to your own husbands; that, if any obey not the word, they also may without the word be won by the conversation of the wives; While they behold your chaste conversation coupled with fear. Whose adorning let it not be that outward adorning of plaiting the hair, and of wearing of gold, or of putting on of apparel; But let it be the hidden man of the heart, in that which is not corruptible, even the ornament of a meek and quiet spirit, which is in the sight of God of*

The Angle Of Comparison

great price. For after this manner in the old time the holy women also, who trusted in God, adorned themselves, being in subjection unto their own husbands: Even as Sara obeyed Abraham, calling him lord: whose daughters ye are, as long as ye do well, and are not afraid with any amazement. Likewise, ye husbands, dwell with them according to knowledge, giving honor unto the wife, as unto the weaker vessel, and as being heirs together of the grace of life; that your prayers be not hindered" (1 Pet. 3:1-7).

Note: Admiration is different from comparison. Admiration concentrates on oneself while comparison involves two different persons. You can learn and emulate what is good from the other person as long as it brings peace, harmony and moves your family forward. When God is involved in a marriage, it cannot fail.

Your Marriage Like No Other

Chapter Three

Why Marriages And Families Are Different

The first family God made by Himself, Mr. and Mrs. Adam was different from the families that follow after such as the families of Cain, Seth, Enoch, Noah, etc. And this is made possible for many reasons.

We have a short time on earth. Therefore, tell God to teach you to number your days. Psalms 90: 12 says, "So teach us to number our days, that we may apply our hearts unto wisdom." Peace is a non-negotiable factor in our homes if we want to live and see good days. As long as there is life, give peace a chance and never allow anger to linger.

"Be ye angry, and sin not: let not the sun go down upon your wrath" (Eph. 4:26).

Anger and impatience are destructive, and if allowed, they can pull done a great house.

Marriage is in phases that keep evolving as the couple keeps unfolding and coming closes to each other. It is a journey, and it takes time to become one in marriage.

There are both physical and spiritual influences that affect the marriage such as spirit spouse, faulty foundation including ancestral spirits, negative covenants, curses, negative family altars, idolatry, etc. All these things whether we know them or not make a lot of difference in our families. They result in attacks, ill health, barrenness and all forms of limitations in marriage thereby turning our joy into mourning. Understand these opposing forces and deal with them decisively in prayer. How much we have dealt with them makes a lot of difference in our marriage as ignorance of these keep one's family in the dark and in prison.

There Are Differences In Marriage As A Result Of :

Level of knowledge: This differs from one family to another, some married as friends while some married by recommendation. They got to know themselves in the marriage so they don't know much about the upbringing,

Why Marriages And Families Are Different

belief, interest, philosophy and previous experiences like rape, abortion and early experiences of their spouse which may take a big toll on the marriage after that. In some families, these things are kept secret while in some they are revealed. More so where a man married a teen with the view to training her, their knowledge levels differ.

Foundation Differences: These are early experiences encountered by the individual, from the day of conception and the environment in which he or she is brought up in. Some children due to tradition, culture and religious background are presented to idols, dedicated to altars and water spirits, while some have pure biblical background void of any fetish and ungodly ancestral worship. These two marriages and families cannot be the same.

> *"If the foundations are destroyed, what can the righteous do?" (Psalms 11:3).*

The upbringing of these righteous families ensures that they enjoy grace and divine favor in their endeavours, and eat the fruits of the labor of their fathers. For the seed of the righteous shall be mighty in the land according to Psalm 112, while the other family's upbringing creates a lot of obstacles, ups, and downs, struggles, backwardness, and limitations in their endeavours, etc. The differences are clear.

Some people are born out of wedlock. Due to this foundation of rejection, their lifestyle and behaviour reflect in their marriages. Unlike a child born in proper marriage, loved and cherished by everyone, the results are not the same. However, with wisdom and knowledge, you can build to last. Your marriage can work if you work on it. Know the foundation of your spouse. Know the environment where your spouse is coming from. These play a big role in the life of a person. The early life experience has a lot to do with a person's later life.

Family Lifestyle/Approach: Family lifestyles differ from one family to another. Some adopt a laissaz-faire approach; some are democratic, while others are autocratic. In a laissaz faire approach; the parent does not care what the children are doing, they have what they demand, and do whatever they feel like doing and are pampered by everyone.

Democratic Approach: In a democratic approach; the parent gives room for everyone to participate and take responsibility. There is freedom of speech and expression. The rights of every member of the family are respected regardless of age differences. Children are encouraged to participate in decision making and express their creativity, though with the sense of submission to the authority of the parent. It does not encourage rebellion and against authority but upholds the rule of law.

Why Marriages And Families Are Different

Autocratic Approach: This approach allows the man or woman to dominate the leadership of the family while others are like subjects. He makes the decision unilaterally. Nobody has the right to air his/her view or make contributions to the well-being of the family. There is not much warmth, love, creativity, and initiative from the children in many cases. The father has no time to relate to the children, and they grow on their own, in most cases, they become rebellious, violent and aggressive. This autocratic approach makes their family like no other.

Marriage and the family is teamwork, and we should approach it with that understanding. God designed the family unit to function as a team. He created us for connection, not for isolation. We are going to explore some benefits of teamwork to expatiate the need for teamwork in our marriages and families. God always performs His work wherever there is synergy.

BENEFITS OF TEAMWORK

1 It multiplies results

2. It decreases loneliness

3. It allows friendships to develop

5. It distributes and shares responsibilities

4. It increases the chance of accuracy of decision

5. It releases the talents and strengths of everyone

3. It provides emotional, psychological and spiritual protection for every member of the family

QUALITIES OF A TEAM PLAYER

1. **Commitment:** The difference between involvement and commitment is a sacrifice. Commitment is the willingness to pay the prize to achieve a goal.

2. **Flexibility:** Willingness to change. When team members are rigid, the team will break up.

3. **Cooperation:** Putting heads together for success. It is not about me but us.

4. **Compliments:** In teamwork complimenting one another is better than competing with one another.

5. **Communication:** This is like the engine oil that lubricates the team. It means to be open. Everybody has information on what to do and does it all the time.

6. **Humility:** When you are humble, you esteem other members of your team higher than yourself.

7. **Discipline:** Every member of the family should exercise good control over their thoughts and emotions. It helps you do what you have to do and not what you want to do.

Why Marriages And Families Are Different

Assuming a child suffered rejection from early childhood experience, it will affect his/her spouse and possibly the children if not properly dealt with. There was a case where a woman suffered rape as a child, and this reflected in her marriage, years after. During sex, she always assumed that the man lying with her is as cruel as the man that raped her many years ago. As a result, she would always push her husband away during sexual intercourse. Unfortunately, the family suffered from it. Though, it may not be the same in every other marriage. Remember, your marriage is like no other.

Give your children and family attention. Teach them to be strong in the face of trouble. From the womb let the child feel loved and important. The absence of love negatively affects behaviour even as an adult, and one's spouse suffers most.

Praise your children and stay with them, it makes them feel encouraged and confident when they are out of the house. Companionship and friendship given to a child at home make him/her a top achiever in later life.

OTHER REASONS WHY YOURS IS LIKE NO OTHER

Mental Intelligence differs from family to family: Our IQ is not the same. Learning speed and the rate of assimilation differ from person to person and from family to family.

The Financial Level Of Both Spouses Makes Marriage Different: Consider the father's and a mother's financial level. High or low-income family background makes marriage differ.

Environment Factor Makes Families Differ: When children are raised up in an environment of affluence, where they are pampered with money, often times, they struggle with integrity, diligence and hard-work. Most of them end up living extravagant lifestyle, with total disregard for financial prudence and discipline, especially if the money is ill-gotten.

Position In The Family: Firstborns are mostly attached to their extended families. The only son, the last born, children born out of wedlock make marriage different.

Genetic Factors Also Affect Marriage: Genetics is what you inherited from your parents. Heredity is a biological process where a parent passes certain genes onto their children or offspring. The study of heredity has shown that the characteristics of living things are transmitted from one generation to the next. These genetic materials make up our DNA molecules play significant roles in our everyday life. Just as the genetic constitution of an individual organism is different, so is the genetic constitution of every family.

Temperament Makes Marriage Different: Since temperament is commonly defined as the manner of thinking, behaving,

Why Marriages And Families Are Different

or reacting characteristic of a specific person, it is obviously a significant component of our lives. Our temperaments differ, and we carry it into our marriages. These aspects of our individual personalities that are often regarded as innate rather than learned, affects our marriages greatly.

Social Skills: Those that lack social skills make marriage different. Exposure differs from level to level. When you find out the level of your family's social skills, you can work on it and move on with your life.

Academic Attainment Makes Marriage Different: Some people have a better understanding. They assimilate before they undertake. Couples' understanding differs, and most times it affects their children. If you work in ignorance, everybody suffers it. Some people understand faster than others. We have to embrace these realities of life and compliments each other.

Interest: Emotional factors and interest differs. The value we place on things differs. What interest you may not be what interest your spouse, therefore, know and harmonize your the differences to build a solid home for your family to thrive. Remember, your marriage is like no other.

The Behavioral Pattern Differs: Families differ in the way they see and reason about things. Most people born out of wedlock have a psychological defect. You need to treat them differently from others with caution and respect. Some keep secrets while others don't. Some are introvert others extrovert. Find out a convenient time for discussion, sex, play, feeding, etc.

Vision: In some homes, the man may be more observant and visionary, while in some homes the woman does. It takes understanding for your marriage to work. It takes wisdom and proper adjustment and discernment to make a marriage work. Your marriage is like no other. Work on it. No marriage is destined to fail.

Visitation Differs: Time for God's visitation differs. No one in a family or marriage determines their time of visitation but God does whatever pleases Him, and no one can question Him. Psalms 115:3 says, *"But our God is in the heavens: he hath done whatsoever he hath pleased."*

Relationship Differs: Love language and relational attitude differ from family to family. People differ in the way they express and receive affection. Some husbands express their love openly with excitement while some do not have such an attitude towards their spouse. We have introvert and extrovert responses.

Why Marriages And Families Are Different

Sharing Responsibility In Family Differs: There are families where only the man brings money while in the other families both or even the woman can finance the bills. Know what works best for your family.

Career Choices Differ: There are families where their children are at the mercy of the housemaid. The parent leaves to work in the morning and comes back late in the night. Due to their career, the children suffer while in some family the woman may choose to resign from work and raise the children.

Types of family: ***Monogamy, Polygamy, Single Parenting, Polyandry, and Bigamy:***

- Monogamy is a family structure where a man has only one wife and children if any.

- Polygamy is a family structure where a man has more than one wife.

- Polyandry is a family structure where a woman has more than one husband; this is rare in our time.

- Single parenting is a family structure where a single parent raises the children as a result of either, divorce, death; widow or widower, single or unmarried women or men having children out of wedlock.

- Bigamy is the crime of marrying a person while already legally married to someone else.

All these family structures and more make marriage/family unique, like no other.

Decision Style: There are places where it is only one person that can make a decision. It may be the man or the woman. When a woman is given an opportunity to make decisions, she should regard it as a privilege and exercise it with respect and humility. In other cases, some spouses make the decision together even involving their children where necessary.

Choice Differs: We make choices for different reasons, and it affects so many things and also differs from family to family. Make valuable choices. Choice of words, choice of action, choice of location, personal appearance, business, house, etc. differ and makes a marriage like no other. See how Esau's choice of wife and Jacob's choice in the Bible differ. Some marry from the same faith, culture, tribe, and tradition while some marry from a different ethnic group, faith, tribe, culture, and tradition. It makes their marriage unique, like no other.

Investment And Banking Issues Differ: Some couples have joint accounts while some don't. Some make investments in their own their names while some make them in their children's name.

Why Marriages And Families Are Different

Treatment Towards Extended Family Relation Differs: Some treat family issues together. Example: they equally share extended families financial and welfare responsibilities. While in some families either the man or the woman's family is the focus while the other extended family suffers in neglect.

Values Differ: Some family place value on their children's education while others place more value on their relatives or investments. The value we put on food, house appliances, furniture, clothes and personal appearance differs from family to family.

Location Differs: Don't compare families in Europe, Asia, or America with families in Nigeria or this part of the world. Their way of reasoning, their exposure and their environment, differ. Making such comparison is an inversion of reality. What works here might not be socially acceptable there.

Close And Open Family Systems: Some families divulge information easily than others. In a close family, information is held in secret while in an open family they share their information with their friends.

Income Level: Salaries of spouses differ, in some home the woman may earn higher than the man or even in business, their income levels may differ. This disparity makes a lot of difference in their decision and character disposition. Know your status especially when you are payroll earners. Spend according to your salary and don't always go out to compete with each other or with others.

Stress Management: Some families manage stress better than others. Others break apart in times and seasons of crises.

Application Of Principles Differs: One should be careful about how he or she applies teachings and seminars on marriage and other subjects. The principles may be the same, but the application differs because of family differences. What is acceptable in your marriage may not be acceptable in the other person's marriage. Therefore, apply the principles the manner it will work for you to ensure peace, harmony, and lasting prosperity.

Raising Godly Seeds Means Different Things To Different Families: To some families to be godly is to make sure the child pass through their religious rights, traditions and to fulfill their church obligations while raising godly seeds in some families entails laying godly foundation through the revelation of God's word and a godly lifestyle as an example to follow.

"For where envy and self-seeking exist, confusion and every evil thing are there" **(James 3:16, NKJV).**

Chapter Four

Understanding Factor

The levels of understanding in families differ. Also the levels of application of wisdom and knowledge differ from one family to another. How we apply these virtues in families determines whether the marriage will work or not. Due to the lack of practical application of these virtues, so many people have suffered in marriage. Consequently, it looks like widowhood is preferred than being married.

We need the seven spirits described in the book of Isaiah 11:2 to guide us into God's pattern of family.

> *"And the spirit of the LORD shall rest upon him, the spirit of wisdom and understanding, the spirit of counsel and might, the spirit of knowledge and of the fear of the LORD"* (KJV).

Let's briefly look at the spirit of wisdom: You cannot do anything with lasting values in the family ministry except these seven spirits are in place. The spirit of wisdom helps one to interpret and apply knowledge correctly. The scripture says that wisdom is the principle thing. Wisdom is built to last. That is why the Bible says a wise woman builds her house. It makes one wise-hearted in decision making, anger management and in crises. Wisdom is a good manager. May God put wisdom in you as He put in the life of Aholiab.

> *"And I, behold, I have given with him Aholiab, the son of Ahisamach, of the tribe of Dan: and in the hearts of all that are wise hearted, I have put wisdom, that they may make all that I have commanded thee"* (Exo.31:6).

Friend, if you lack wisdom on how to manage your home ask the Lord. The Bible says,

> *"If any of you lack wisdom, let him ask of God, that giveth to all men liberally, and upbraideth not; and it shall be given him"* (James 1:5).

Another factor is the spirit of understanding: Understanding is defined as the ability to assimilate before undertaking. This

Understanding Factor

definition connotes having an understanding of previous and present situations and being able to take the right action. Some people have a quick understanding, and some don't. You need the spirit of understanding to know your spouse and children's aspirations, needs, temperament, behaviors, and their desires per time.

A lady told me "mommy, I hate men." I asked her why and she said: "I was raped as a child." That was the reason why she resents men at this stage in her life. We must endeavour to interpret people's behavior in the light of the spirit of understanding. The stimulus (Cause and Effect) motivates every reaction. Understanding each person's make up makes a difference in every home.

Lately, I have had a series of calls and witnessed people that the pressures of marriages has reduced to a crush of bread. May the spirit of understanding deliver you from this ugly experience and trauma befalling many in these perilous times we live in. Most men and women have lost their focus and identity in the course of marriage crises.

If you take a look into so many marriages, you will realize that so many people are tired of their marriages. The whole issue here is that we have refused to understand our marriages. Two of you have different backgrounds, early childhood experiences, and upbringing, purposes, lifestyles, aspirations, different approaches to life, etc. Every spouse should look into their marriage and find out what it needs and what is lacking. Once it is supplied, and necessary adjustments are made the family moves on again.

There should be no comparison in marriage. Understanding is very important. No two marriages are the same. Even siblings have different marriage patterns and understanding modes.

There was a time that some ministers were preaching about spouse joint account. A woman that owns a school went and opened a joint account with her husband and put all the school's money. Later on, the husband went and withdrew all the money without the woman's knowledge to solve his own problem. The woman later found out that there is no money to pay her workers. She collapsed. She forgot that the application of these principles differs. Most times there is a difference in the application and interpretation of God's word based on knowledge of each family. My dear, wisdom is the principle thing. It guides you in the application of knowledge. If your wife is an extravagant spending type trusting family finances into her hands is a tragedy, but a manager of wealth can save the family from financial embarrassment. Assuming your spouse is a drunkard, and a womanizer (God forbids)

Understanding Factor

who enjoys wasteful spending, running joint account is a risk. Marriage counselors should be wise and deal with each family according to their uniqueness. Every marriage is unique, like no other.

Everyone that entered into the marriage institution has good intention and desires a happy marriage, but this expectation fails most times because of lack of understanding. Take time to study your marriage and be patient to see that things work out as desired.

What every spouse needs is God for without Him there will be no success, joy, and peace at home. A prayerless man and woman is a recipe for failure, not only in marriage but life in general as believers. He gives power, counsel and might to stay together until the season of rain, flood and wind are over. By strength shall no man prevail but only by His spirit.

> *"Then he answered and spake unto me, saying, This is the word of the LORD unto Zerubbabel, saying, Not by might, nor by power, but by my spirit, saith the LORD of hosts"* (Zech. 4:6).

Knowledge of God delivers you from anxiety, pressure, presumptuousness and emotional imbalance. For instance, going through your spouse's phone, witch hunting and unnecessary supervision, will rather ruin your marriage.

Naturally, some men are very sociable and extrovert. When they go out in public places women like them and admire them. Most times those women that admire such men can give them contracts, business connections or even ordinary airtime and other good things without demanding anything in return. If your husband has such disposition, don't feel threatened and hinder those opportunities that can potentially be a blessing to the family. All you need is more understanding of how to manage the situation. The same applies to the wife. Let your prayers and spirit of understanding fight your battles instead of ruining it with your own hands.

One thing that makes a difference in marriage is the level of understanding between spouses. First of all, the level of their understanding of their love for God and the level of their understanding of God's purpose for their spouse, marriage, and family. Also important is the level of their understanding of how your spouse sees things as well as understanding about your spouse's background. If we lack these levels of understanding of these areas of our marital lives, it will create w vacuum that the pressure of the world will attempt to fill, because life does not permit a vacuum.

Assuming Joel came from a wealthy family and his wife is from a low-income family with little resources to meet the basic needs of life. This social disparity in their family background can be a source of problem in their marriage if not practical harmonized. Example: whenever he gives you (the wife) money for family upkeep, she may want to be frugal in her spending because of her background. As a result, she ends up not spending commensurately to justify the amount the husband provides. So, when serves him the food at his table there isn't much meat and condiments, he may endure it but for a while but tomorrow he may want to eat outside the home. This is because she fails to acknowledge that her husband is from a wealthy family that has experienced affluence as a young person all through his life.

Some were brought up by a single parent, some grew up as a servant or apprentice, and some are from a low-income family. If you don't know the background of your spouse, there will be a lot of frustration in the marriage. Who is his father and who is his mother? Did he have parental love? A man without parental love answers you with violence. An attempt to love him or show him love will make him feel deceived and cheated. Every of his action is "by force." Therefore, understand him, he means well, regardless of how he expresses it.

Some men see a woman as a second-class citizen and only a helper or assistance but not as their bone. He does not see you as his soul mate or lover. He does not see you as a friend. Rather he sees you as a property he paid for to be reproducing children for him. So, at this level, he values his children more than you. You mean nothing much to him. Some of those men collect their wives' salary and leave them with nothing so that they will beg them for every need and they are happy about it. Your marriage is unique.

Understand his academic and mental intelligence level. Know how he reasons and perceives issues. Educational exposure upgrades one's reasoning and also affects behavior. Understanding your spouse's academic and mental level makes you manage his or her downsides more easily and moderates one's expectations.

> *"And of the children of Issachar, which were men that had understanding of the times, to know what Israel ought to do; the heads of them were two hundred; and all their brethren were at their commandment" (I1Chron. 12:32).*

Note: The children of Issachar knew the right action to take because of understanding. Under the earth there are times and seasons, know what your spouse and children need at every particular season and time in their lives. Right action results in a right response. Some women's seasons may be times of nagging, anger and provocative words, and an understanding man at this point knows the right thing to do and once he does it everybody and everything will be under his command. No need to fuel the fire, everybody enjoys harmony, peace, and joy which should be the target of every family.

When one party in the family is happy, enjoying and celebrating and the other is mourning, sorrowing and weeping, you should not ignore it; if you do, something is wrong. That marriage is not successful, and it depicts a lack of understanding. So, seek for the joy of every member of the family, and you will eat the fruits shortly. Your marriage cannot work until you work on it.

Embrace the spirit of understanding. You will be ten times better and understand the uniqueness of your marriage.

> *"And in all matters of wisdom and understanding, that the king enquired of them, he found them ten times better than all the magicians and astrologers that were in all his realm" (Dan. 1:20).*

Your Marriage Like No Other

Chapter Five

Issues Of Submission

The concept of submission is view differently based on culture, tradition, physiology, vision, religion, and upbringing. In some cultures, submission means subjugation, slavery, and imprisonment of the woman. The woman in that family is worthless; her price is less than a penny. She has nothing meaningful to contribute to the family. She is confined at home to breed and raise children up, cook for the family and do the house chores. "She is in the inner room" imprisoned, neglected and abandoned. She is only needed when the man desires her. In such families and culture, the woman has no right to earn a salary, own properties or exercise her civic right, etc.

Churches, cultures, and traditions differ. Some churches do not allow their women to speak publicly. They should only ask questions at home. Their purpose on earth is towards their husband, children, and home, nothing beyond that. Most women from this background are bottled up. They merely endure marriage; they live an unfulfilled life, they lack expression and feel unloved. I have seen homes like that, where the primary purpose of women is to take care of the husband, children, and home alone.

In some cultures and teachings, each person is respected. The woman is a participant in church and at home. The husband even helps the woman in raising the children and lifts off some burdens from her at home. These families have redefined submission. They help one another to fulfill their purpose in God. The place of the men is acknowledged, as well as the women's. No extreme left or right. A balance is drawn, and things are working well. Most times preachers and teachers of marriage and relationships teach based on their experience and understanding of biblical interpretation, not acknowledging the fact that their marriage is not like others, and what works for them may not work for others.

Issues Of Submission

The interpretation of a subject in the scripture is most times based on the teacher's understanding, experience, vision, perspective, background, and revelation, etc. Impressing it on other people can potentially cause lots of pain, regret, and separation. A lot of women have been mentally, physically, emotionally and psychologically abused and tortured because of the matter of submission. Love plus submission produces desirable results for anyone that wants his family to work. Draw a balance and let each person's potential be accessed as this increases the family's output.

We are in the 21st century; career women are out there grappling with the challenges associated with their carer even as mothers. At times stopping them from their jobs has worked for some families but to some, it has resulted in crises, poverty, and regret. So know what works for you and stick to it. Let love be without dissimulation.

> "Let love be without dissimulation. Abhor that which is evil; cleave to that which is good" (Rom 12:9).

Many times, when the man experiences a financial setback and retrenchment, the woman's income becomes a big comfort and a cover to the entire family till the man bounces back. Submission is strength, power, and influence put under control. She is under control to accommodate the leadership of the husband. Once a woman does this, she wins at home and occupies the heart of the husband. Submission done in the atmosphere of hatred and humiliation is like hard and prostrated labor. The woman does it under compulsion and sadness although she may not express it for the sake of peace. But once she has her liberty, she reveals her real person in action. When submission is expressed under an atmosphere of love and respect, it produces an ambiance at home that brings the best out of the woman and everyone in the family.

Once a man finds out that the woman has not come to struggle or usurp his position in the family, but to reverent and willing submits, then he releases his heart/head for her (the neck) to turn it around. At this level of maturity, both submit to each other, and there is nothing to be apprehensive of, his heart is safely trusted in her.

> *"The heart of her husband doth safely trust in her so that he shall have no need of spoil. She will do him good and not evil all the days of her life" (Pro. 31:11-12).*

No man thrusts his heart in the hand of a woman that does not recognize, respect and establish his leadership at home. There is rest in a home where the family organogram is rightly positioned (Father, Mother, and Children). A sweet and happy home is not built in a day.

Ladies, know what submission means to your husband and allow him to define it for you, but use understanding and wisdom to turn it in the right direction. Marriage is a school you never graduate from. Learn through your marriage experiences and determined to make it work. If you do, God will help you and crown your genuine efforts with visible and enduring success.

Finally, let every man love his wife as Christ loved the Church and let every woman submit to her husband in all things. Treat each other as friends, soul mates, life partners, sisters, brothers and let the joy of one be the joy of another, accepting each other for who they are, not being ashamed of each other but working to make the other be his or her best. Also, help each other to fulfill their God-given purpose in life and never allow selfishness to ruin your relationship. Other people will eventually go at some point; children, friends, and extended families, etc. leaving only the two of you (The husband and wife). So treat each other with utmost care, respect, warmth, compassion, praising each other and strengthening your area of strength ignoring flaws, drawbacks, and weaknesses.

Seeing that the two of you have a limited time to live here on earth, make every effort to enjoy yourselves. Make good use of your time, stay healthy together and let your children grow to see the two of you as a great inspiration.

If you are separated, single parent, widow or widower whatever be your situation, make yourself happy, fulfill the purpose of God for your life, eat good food to live long. Shun anxiety, worry, and frustration.

Chapter Six

Tidy Up Your Home

Make adequate use of the opportunity you have as a family to be together. Everyone has a part to play for peace to reign in your home. Families are dynamic and evolve from season to season.

Don't Compare Families
- Know the season your family is in and look for a strategy to make the best out of it.

- A winner at home seems to be the weak person; it is rather a wise display of strength.

- Teach your children and every member of the family how to act responsibly. All should share responsibility in the family.

- Perception and characters differ. In a family where there is the spirit of understanding, there will be moderate temperament.

- Understanding that your family is a pattern or model your children will exhibit one day and somewhere.

- Relationship building is a responsibility that everyone must take.

- If you don't have a relationship with your children, they will go out to look for it. So show them that you love them sincerely.

- Understand that what people are looking for in life are joy and fulfillment.

- Moderate your thoughts before speaking or acting, and you will avoid mistakes.

- The spirit of understanding helps you to know that your family is like no other and will guide you to know what to do at all times.

- Understanding helps you to think properly.

- Understanding will help you to coordinate your affairs well and also regulate your attitude.

- People around interpret us. They want to know how your family is doing. So do everything to give them a reason to interpret well to the glory of God.

Don't rule out and be dismissive when people complain about you; it is a way of showing you who you are. God can speak to you through an insult, a rebuke, criticism, etc. Just learn from it and move forward with your life.

Your Home Is A Place Of Rest

Find out the rough and bumpy parts.

Find out what causes disagreements and avoid it

Point of distress: know when he or she is in distress.

Avoid nagging.

Give peace and time to your spouse for them to mature.

Find out time for discussions, sex, etc.

Give time for the rage or anger to subside.

Find out whom your spouse is; his/her position, grace, behavioral pattern, etc.

If Your Family Is Not Well-Coordinated You Will Not Live For Long:

- Focus on the strengths and leave the weaknesses of your spouse and children.

- With the power of prayer and corresponding action, change what is wrong with your family.

- To maintain joy is a fight. Guide your mind.

- Be with people of like mind.

- Forgive whoever offends you.

Marriage is a house under construction. It is a difficult venture, but a wise woman and man keep building until it becomes a perfect house. We should be wise not to tear your home by our foolishness. For a family to function well, somebody must pay the price. Avoid divorce by all means; it does not just happen. So tackle it at the earlier stage with tolerance and love.

Some things can lead to divorce such as accumulated offences, words, dress code, infidelity, dirtiness, etc., so be mindful of them and address them immediately. Avoid doing what your spouse keeps warning you about or dislikes.

Things To Do To Avoid Divorce

- Avoid offences and correct what your spouse is complaining about.

- Buy peace at all costs.

- Humble yourself to save your marriage.

- Say I am sorry at the right time.

- Make relevant sacrifices to keep your home.

- Avoid being hurtful and seeking revenge.

- Fight with it from the spiritual point of view. You can go for deliverance at the right place, seek counseling from a balanced and wise pastor.

- When the journey gets tough, go on your knees and plead. It's better to sell pride and shame than allowing divorce. There is hope in every home where the wife is a praying woman.

- Understand that men always yield to those who give them respect.

- Know the libido of your spouse and satisfy him/her, never abuse this.

- Generally, it is the woman who holds the key to the peace in the home, but in some homes, it is the man.

- Avoid being jealous and think about the other person wellbeing first.

- Never leave the Holy Spirit behind. He is the major instructor in marriage

- Build your prayer life, allow the Holy Spirit take over

- Develop a personal, fervent prayer life; the greatest weapon in a woman's life is prayer. No man no matter how strong can resist prayers.

Use prayer to change your spouse's habit and even your children's. Prayer has so much impact, as long as your marriage is built on God.

When you avoid divorce, your children will benefit from it now, and in the future. Otherwise, the marriage of your children will also reflect it. They will unconsciously carry it over to their homes.

- Remove every form of selfishness

- Prefer one another over all others

- An effective prayer life can displace stubbornness

Application Of Principles Of Marriage

- Use only workable systems.
- Know whom you married.
- Don't place your family below others.
- Collectively, always try to make your marriage work.
- Handle banking issues with precaution.
- Carefully manage family secrets.
- Let everything be done out of love, peace and for the betterment of the entire family.
- Find out how your spouse appreciates you and take it that way. Don't bug him/her with other people's methods of appreciation.
- Life is a choice; run from provocations and outbursts of anger.
- Anything you tackle with the word of God will never raise its head again.
- Be mindful of family godly culture and never abandon it at all for any reason.
- Value peace more than anything else.
- Look and be mindful of the family value system.

- There is wisdom in keeping the peace of the home.

- Marriage is a school, and everyone must adjust to ensure success.

- Find out what your marriage needs and provide it.

- Make your home a paradise; pay the price, and you will reap in due time. It will give you space to travel in the spirit.

- Always work towards your health for self-preservation.

- Correcting each other at the point of mistakes doesn't give a good result. So look for proper time for corrections.

- No man will want a woman to lead him. But you can lead your husband based on your submission. Submission is a display of maturity.

- Apply strength. Strength is the ability to resolve any issue without breaking.

Peace is a process; patiently work it out. It doesn't come in one day. The peace and joy of every home are dependent on the knowledge and understanding of both the spouses, so go for knowledge.

Tidy Up Your Home

The spirit of understanding makes you move your family forward. Understanding people's temperaments is important and it always consider the interest of the other person.

Don't break the flow of communication. Bridge the gap if you observe any. Although communication differs from family to family, know how best both of you flow in communication.

- Marriage should be a friendship boat. You are what you hear so be careful what you hear and how you absorb it.

- Run away from revenge; it is a very dangerous tool.

- Allow your marriage to flow from the Holy Spirit, for the kingdom of God is already in you.

- Try to relate to God on a personal level because He is your personal God.

- Have a team spirit; even God is not a lone ranger for He is relational.

- Place value on every member of your family.

- Any gift you receive is for the benefit of the family.

Your body is not your own so don't defraud, withhold, or deprive your partner of his or her rights. If a situation looks defrauding, deal with it immediately and ask for forgiveness.

> *"You cry out, "Why doesn't the Lord accept my worship?" I'll tell you why! Because the Lord witnessed the vows you and your wife made when you were young. But you have been unfaithful to her, though she remained your faithful partner, the wife of your marriage vows. Didn't the Lord make you one with your wife? In body and spirit you are his. And what does he want? Godly children from your union. So guard your heart; remain loyal to the wife of your youth. For I hate divorce!" says the Lord, the God of Israel. "To divorce your wife is to overwhelm her with cruelty,]" says the Lord of Heaven's Armies. "So guard your heart; do not be unfaithful to your wife" (Malachi 2:14-16 NLT).*

Chapter Seven

My Story

This book came as a result of my experience and leadership amongst woman for close to four decades. Marriage like no other applies to every individual and people. No family in African, Europe, and Asia shares the same marriage tradition and philosophy. Even in the same nation, family system and marriage patterns are not the same. Many factors are responsible to this.

I grew up in the Body of Christ when there were few marriages. The concentration then was on evangelism and revival. Little attention was given to building marriages and relationships. Few sisters that married then portrayed a picture of distress, lack, regret, and sadness. Those sisters previously were zealous and manifested gifts of the Holy Ghost which later seem subdued after marriage.

Their complaints were unending and regretful, which made most of us dread and feared getting married. In response to this development that is at variance with the scriptures, I entered into a season of prayer to escape this plague that portrayed marriage as a burial ground for one's grace, zeal, fervent love for the Lord, and calling. I took a serious responsibility and resolved not to be a victim of such an anomaly at the time. This is what inspired the formation of Potter's House Women Fellowship, International, and her offshoots.

Most of my friends bought into the vision and we started praying earnestly. As we persisted and remained focused, many women joined us from different parts of the world. Today, Potter's House Women Fellowship International, raises, teaches and trains women to believe that no matter your story as a woman, wife, and sister in the course of the marriage and the family journey you can rise against all odd in the face of adversity, and still fulfill your purpose in God. No matter how shattered you are, battered, abused, pushed out and humiliated by drugs, emotional abuse, persistent failure, disappointments and deprivations, the Potter can fix you up again. Testimonies abound on this. Our teachings equip and empower the woman, girl child, and all youth, in general, to be impactful, live a meaningful, happy, productive and fulfilled life, as a woman.

All these success stories and testimonies would have been a mirage if we did not appreciate the uniqueness of our union as husband and wife. The ministry platform and leadership experience had taught me patience and longsuffering, which has helped my marriage to mature quickly. It has enhanced my spiritual life because people look up to me as a model, so I die daily bringing my body under subjection not to disappoint their expectations, seeing it as a challenge and an obligation to live up to what I preach. My marriage is a reference point like no other, a lot of sacrifices is invested in making the marriage work.

> *"But I keep under my body, and bring it into subjection: lest that by any means, when I have preached to others, I myself should be a castaway" (1 Cor. 9:27).*

I have been challenged from time to time to raise the standard of this ministry from one level to the other thereby imbibing the culture of discipline and hard work. My husband and the family benefits from these adjustments to make us great as never before. While in other families is not the case and can perhaps never be tolerated.

My husband's marriage proposal did not take us unaware; through prayers, we were guided, and events were divinely orchestrated to make the dream come true. In the course of our courtship, he told me that God told him to marry me and said I am going to be a blessing to him, yet at that time, there was nothing indicative to that. I did not look like it at all. God went ahead in one of his retreats to show him the future of Potter's House Women Ministry. He believed it and kept it in his heart. Eventually, we got married, wedded and started our life's journey together. Shortly, Potters House Women Fellowship, International was born and started growing by leaps an bounds in the cities and nations, which made our marriage like no other. His support and love for me and the ministry is second to none. There is no competition and pressure in our family because of his knowledge and understanding through the help of the Holy Spirit.

The billboards advertising our citywide conferences have only my photos, unlike the common trend that projects the man or has the photo of both couples. Not all men can allow this. In most cases, I travel alone with other women while some ministers travel together with their spouses. He mapped out days of praying for me, and yet our love and family keeps growing

My Story

positively and expanding. He led me to take the (JAMB) Joint Admission and Matriculation Board entrance exam to the university. His desire for me was to advance my education. Finally, I found myself at the university. After my first degree, he encouraged me to go for a Master's Degree which I did, and now he is encouraging me to undertake my Ph.D. Amazingly, he is less concerned about his academic status. His primary concern is for me to become the best that I can be in ministry, business, relationship and all life endeavours.

How would I not reciprocate by loving, honouring and appreciating such a gift that God has given to humanity? Today, every member of the family is reaping the benefits of the exposure my husband thrust me to gain. He is the catalyst for every good thing that has happened and is happening in our family. The exposure and experiences I have gained over the years have elevated the status of our family. Sadly, some women with greater grace have been flagged down and silenced by their spouses, and the whole family is suffering from such ignorance and egocentric behaviour.

In those days, most men feared this giant step my husband took and expressed their disapproval. They attempted to discourage him by all means, but he was resolute because he was convinced of the revelation he had received from the Lord about our future. Our family and marriage are like no other.

We have a mandate from GOD and day by day it is becoming clearer, transforming and impactful. The testimonies abound in families, lives, institutions, organizations and the nations that God has privileged us to be a blessing to. To God be the glory. I am proud and honoured to be the wife of this rare gem.

In the course of time, I found myself in the midst of families where most women follow their husband and have nothing more to do than to support their husband in ministry. Many of them saw my marriage as not being well-structured, but we understand and support ourselves and live happily, abounding in every good work. Although, times and events are changing their perception and direction towards this issue. We refused to be distracted; our marriage is like no other. Imitating them would have brought a disaster to our family vision, future, and everything about us would have gone down the drain. Potter's House Women Fellowship, our business through which God has nourished us would never have been a story told.

In the course of ministry, I have had the opportunity to meet people, families from different ethnic groups, cultures, nations, etc. and can emphatically say that no two marriages are the same. Both men and women are in different forms, size and shapes so are their behaviors, believes and perceptions.

My Story

Never embrace any teaching, counseling, doctrine that will devastate your marriage, regardless of who preaches it. You have nothing to gain if your home is on fire, and your family is torn apart. Be cautious how you embrace and apply these teachings. Only go for what will keep you incongruent with what the Lord has called your family to do in a way your whole family will enjoy peace and harmony. Your family is like no other.

Your Marriage Like No Other

Reflection

Personal Notes: _____

_____

_____

_____

_____

_____

_____

_____

_____

_____

_____

Guided Action Plan

_____

_____

_____

_____

_____

_____

www.ingramcontent.com/pod-product-compliance
Lightning Source LLC
Chambersburg PA
CBHW032210040426
42449CB00005B/531